JOHN THOMPSON

Third-Grade
VELOCITY STUDIES

Edited and Annotated Versions
of
Standard Dexterity Etudes

5824 **THE WILLIS MUSIC COMPANY**

FOREWORD

The purpose of this book is expressed in its title, i.e., to develop velocity in piano playing of about Third Grade of difficulty. It is designed to supplement the THIRD GRADE BOOK in JOHN THOMPSON'S MODERN COURSE FOR THE PIANO and deals only with the purely technical side of piano playing. All the various phases of pianism have been considered and excellent examples for Right Hand, Left Hand and Hands Together are carefully selected from many of the masters of étude writers.

The editor has given short notes on how to practice each exercise and space is reserved for keeping a record of the velocity attained in each instance.

Needless to say, speed is of no value unless it is under perfect control. Each exercise therefore, should be learned first at slow tempo until accuracy and ease of performance are assured, after which the tempo should be gradually increased.

While the prime purpose of the etudes is to develop the mechanics of piano playing, every effort should be made to play them as artistically as possible. For this reason it is of great importance to observe phrasing, the use of the pedal as indicated and the marks of expression.

John Thompson

W. M. Co. 5824

CONTENTS

– PRACTICE RECORD –

....
(Pupil's Signature)

....
(Teacher's Signature)

Record of Scales and Arpeggios Studied
and Maximum Tempo Attained

═══ SCALES ═══

DATE		TEMPO

══ ARPEGGIOS ══

DATE		TEMPO

– PRACTICE RECORD –

....
(Pupil's Signature)   *(Teacher's Signature)*

Record of Scales and Arpeggios Studied
and Maximum Tempo Attained

DATE	SCALES	TEMPO
	ARPEGGIOS	

Raise and drop the fingers with military precision.

Velocity attained M.M.............

Finger Legato-Right Hand

Czerny

Observe the phrasing and marks of expression.

Velocity attained M.M.............

Finger Legato-Left Hand

Czerny

Use well-articulated finger
legato in both hands.

Velocity attained M.M.............

Finger Legato-Both Hands

Czerny

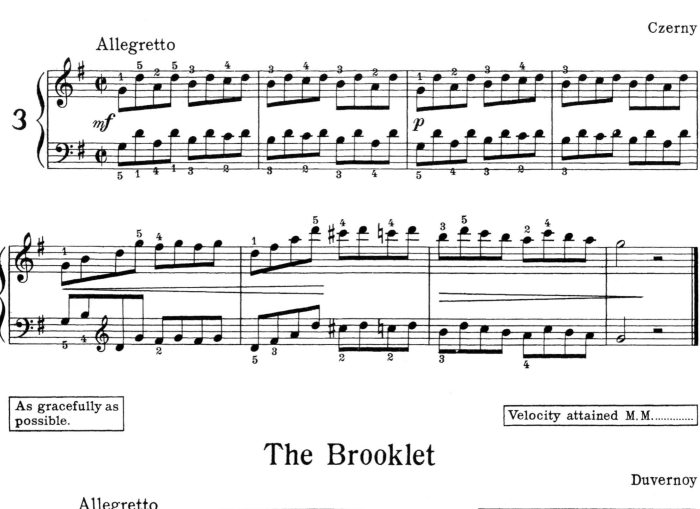

As gracefully as
possible.

Velocity attained M.M.............

The Brooklet

Duvernoy

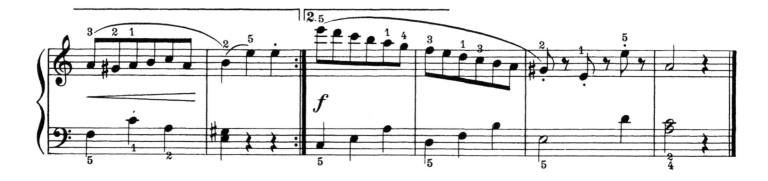

W. M. Co. 5824

Try to play the scales as smoothly as glissandos.

Velocity attained M.M. ....

Legato Scale Passages - Right Hand

Lemoine

Treat the scale figures as an accompaniment to the Melody which should be played as expressively as possible.

Velocity attained M.M.............

Scale figures as Accompaniment

Duvernoy

Velocity attained M. M...............

Wrist Staccato-Right Hand

Czerny

Play the right-hand groups with rolling attack, tossing off the last note of each group.

Velocity attained M. M...............

Rolling Attack-Right Hand

Lemoine

8

Practice first in four-four time.
Later in alla breve.
Apply the swells and diminuendos
as indicated.

Velocity attained M.M.............

Smooth Passage Playing

Le Couppey

Velocity attained M.M............

The Trill

Köhler

Play the scale figures with fingers close to the keys and with a sweeping motion of the arm.
They should sound almost like glissandos.

Velocity attained M.M.............

Diatonic Sweeps

Köhler

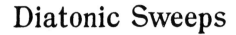

Apply sharp attack and release to the three-note groups in the right hand while the left hand uses a plucking finger staccato.

Velocity attained M.M.............

Three-note Slurs

Czerny

Play the right-hand broken chords with a graceful Rotary Motion. Observe the phrasing of the sustained left hand.

Velocity attained M.M............

Rolling Attack - Broken Chords

Berens

These arpeggio figures should be tossed from one hand to the other and sound as smoothly as though played with one hand.

Velocity attained M.M. ....

By the Seaside

Streabbog

Practice the broken thirds first
with high Finger Legato.
As speed develops, use less and
less finger action.

Velocity attained M.M.............

Broken Thirds

Köhler

Allegretto vivo

Velocity attained M. M.............

Left Hand Broken Chords

Köhler

Roll off the groups in 16ths.
Play the left hand chords with
forearm staccato.

Velocity attained M.M.............

Arabesque

Burgmüller

Play the left hand with strict finger legato – well articulated.

Left Hand Passage Playing

Czerny

18

Play the left hand with close finger legato – employing, at the same time a sweeping motion of the arm.

Velocity attained M.M. ....

March Wind

Czerny

19

Practice this first at moderate tempo with *high finger legato*.
Later, as speed develops, keep the fingers close to the keys and use a rolling motion of the arm.

Velocity attained M.M.............

Broken Chords - Both Hands

Czerny

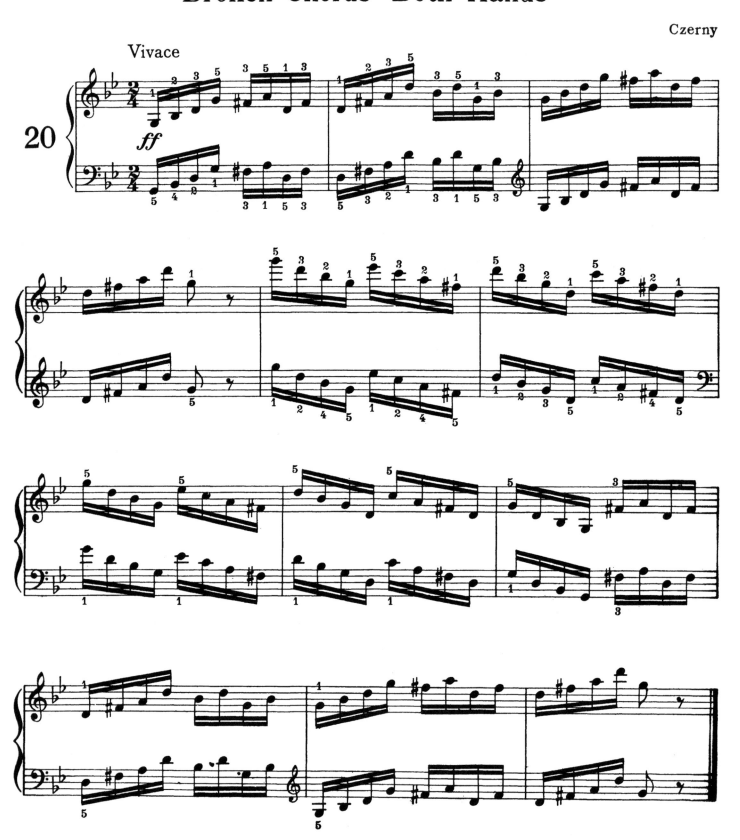

Velocity attained M.M.............

Sustaining the Thumb

Duvernoy

Allegretto

Play the two-note slurs with a
rolling motion of the hand, and
toss off each group sharply.

Velocity attained M.M............

Chasing Butterflies

Streabbog

In the following etude, strive to develop the utmost in smoothness and clarity. Always remember that speed is useless unless it is under perfect control.

Velocity attained M.M. ....

Smoothness in Passage Playing

Köhler, Op. 242

24

Learn this first in four-four time.
Later in alla breve.
Strive for absolute smoothness
and accuracy.

Velocity attained M.M............

Perfect Evenness in Scale Playing *(Right Hand)*

Czerny

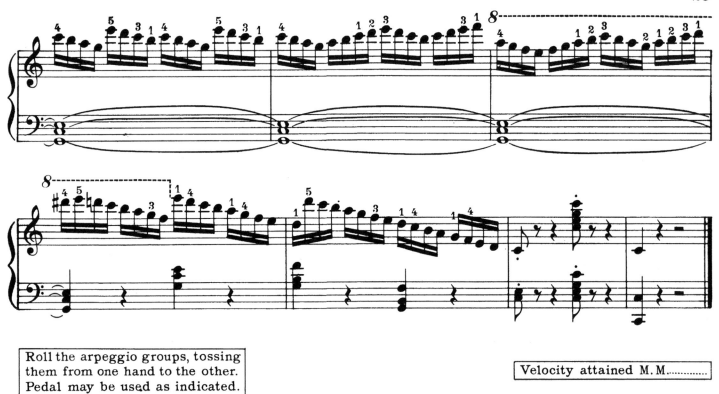

Velocity attained M.M.

Arpeggios divided between the Hands

Czerny

Practice first in four-four time.
Later in alla breve.
Strive for utmost smoothness
and accuracy.

Velocity attained M.M.............

Perfect Evenness in Scale Playing *(Left Hand)*

Czerny

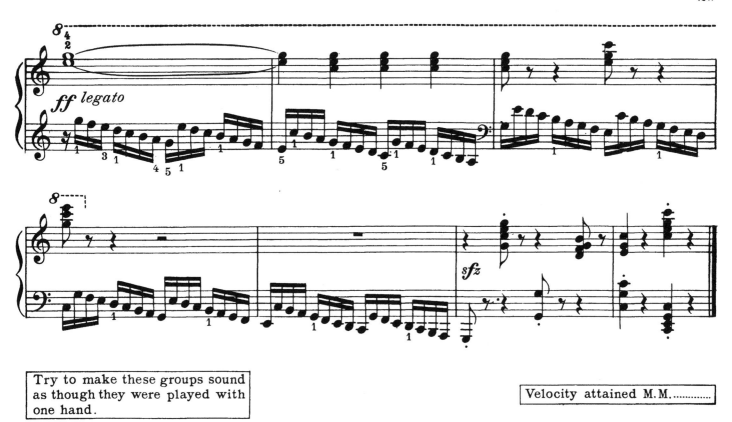

Try to make these groups sound
as though they were played with
one hand.

Velocity attained M.M.............

Broken-Chord Groups

Czerny

Allegro

27

Velocity attained M.M.............

Progress

Burgmüller

Play the chords with arm attack.
Be sure to give a little extra emphasis to
the upper, or melody notes of each chord.
Play the whole etude as musically as
possible.

Velocity attained M.M.............

Album Leaf

Heller

Assai moderato

29

The diatonic groups should be tossed from one hand to the other. Use a slight rolling motion in combination with finger legato to give sparkle.
Play the intervening chords with sharp forearm staccato.

Velocity attained M.M.............

L'avalanche

Heller

Allegro vivace

A study in phrasing.
Follow the phrasing marks exactly and
play with as much artistry as possible.

Velocity attained M.M............

Tender Flower

Burgmüller

A study in Broken Chords.
Observe the notes to be sustained
and pedal as indicated.

Velocity attained M.M..............

Harmonies du Soir

Czerny

Moderato

32

Color rather than speed is essential in this etude.
Play it as musically as possible.

Velocity attained M.M.............

Angel Voices

Burgmüller

Allegro moderato

33

36

Tempo attained M.M.............

Chorale

Duvernoy

Moderato

Velocity attained M.M.............

Fanfare

Duvernoy

Velocity attained M.M.............

Rippling Waters

Czerny

Practice the trill figures first
with high finger action.
As speed develops, the fingers
should be kept closer until they
finally "ride" the keys.

Velocity attained M.M. ....

Carnival of the Birds

Czerny

Allegro

Pedal once to each measure and strive to give a bell-like tone to the accented half-notes.

Velocity attained M.M.............

Criss-Cross

Le Couppey

The Turn.
Play all 32nds with shallow touch.

Velocity attained M.M. ....

Gracefulness

Burgmüller

The C minor Scale used as melody.
Play with as much color as possible.

Velocity attained M.M.............

Prelude

Allegro

Bertini

Use forearm staccato.
Crisp, brittle chords.

Velocity attained M.M.............

Staccato Chord Playing

Lemoine

Velocity attained M.M. ....

Chromatic Scales

Berens

Velocity attained M.M............

Trill Figures

Loeschhorn

Velocity attained M.M.............

Scherzino

Le Couppey

Roll the broken chords.
Play the over-hand stac-
catos with bell-like tone.

Velocity attained M.M.............

The Swallow

Burgmüller

Allegro non troppo

45

Velocity attained M.M. ....

The Turn

Czerny

Give special attention to the Fourth
and Fifth fingers.
Keep the passages perfectly even.

Velocity attained M.M.............

Passage Playing

Köhler

Play with close, bouncing wrist action.

Light Wrist Staccato-Left Hand

Czerny

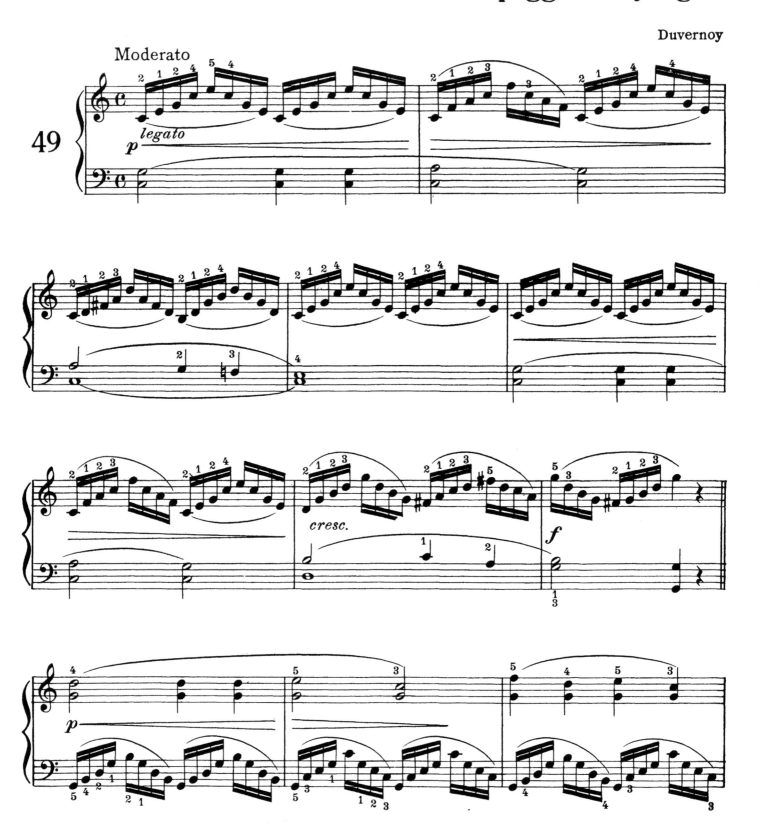

52

Pass the hands over smoothly.
Play with Rolling Attack.

Velocity attained M.M.............

Thumb under and Hand over in Arpeggio Playing

Duvernoy

Velocity attained M.M. ....

Velocity

Duvernoy

Allegro moderato

Writing Exercises for Industrious Students

Chords, Chord Progressions, Cadences, Arpeggios, etc.

Chords, Chord Progressions, Cadences, Arpeggios, etc.

Writing Exercises for Industrious Students
Chords, Chord Progressions, Cadences, Arpeggios, etc.

CLASSICAL PIANO SOLOS

Original Keyboard Pieces from Baroque to the 20th Century

Compiled and edited by Philip Low, Sonya Schumann, and Charmaine Siagian

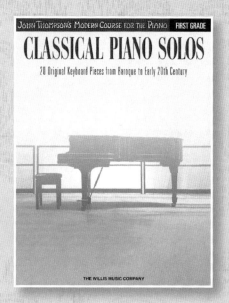

Second Grade

22 pieces: *Bartók*: The Dancing Pig Farmer • *Beethoven*: Ecossaise • *Bonis*: Madrigal • *Burgmüller*: Progress • *Gurlitt*: Etude in C • *Haydn*: Dance in G • *d'Indy*: Three-Finger Partita • *Kirnberger*: Lullaby in F • *Mozart*: Minuet in C • *Petzold*: Minuet in G • *Purcell*: Air in D Minor • *Rebikov*: Limping Witch Lurking • *Schumann*: Little Piece • *Schytte*: A Broken Heart, and more!
00119739 / $6.99

Third Grade

20 pieces: *CPE Bach*: Presto in C Minor • *Bach/Siloti*: Prelude in G • *Burgmüller*: Ballade • *Cécile Chaminade*: Pièce Romantique • *Dandrieu*: The Fifers • *Gurlitt*: Scherzo in D Minor • *Hook*: Rondo in F • *Krieger*: Fantasia in C • *Kullak*: Once Upon a Time • *MacDowell*: Alla Tarantella • *Mozart*: Rondino in D • *Rebikov*: Playing Soldiers • *Scarlatti*: Sonata in G • *Schubert*: Waltz in F Minor, and more!
00119740 / $7.99

Fourth Grade

18 pieces: *CPE Bach*: Scherzo in G • *Teresa Carreño*: Berceuse • *Chopin*: Prelude in E Minor • *Gade*: Little Girls' Dance • *Granados*: Valse Poetic No. 6 • *Grieg*: Arietta • *Handel*: Prelude in G • *Heller*: Sailor's Song • *Kuhlau*: Sonatina in C • *Kullak*: Ghost in the Fireplace • *Moszkowski*: Tarentelle • *Mozart*: Allegro in G Minor • *Rebikov*: Music Lesson • *Satie*: Gymnopedie No. 1 • *Scarlatti*: Sonata in G • *Telemann*: Fantasie in C, and more!
00119741 / $7.99

Fifth Grade

19 pieces: *Bach*: Prelude in C-sharp Major • *Beethoven:* Moonlight sonata • *Chopin*: Waltz in A-flat • *Cimarosa*: Sonata in E-flat • *Coleridge-Taylor*: They Will Not Lend Me a Child • *Debussy*: Doctor Gradus • *Grieg*: Troldtog • *Griffes*: Lake at Evening • *Lyadov*: Prelude in B Minor • *Mozart*: Fantasie in D Minor • *Rachmaninoff*: Prelude in C-sharp Minor • *Rameau*: Les niais de Sologne • *Schumann:* Farewell • *Scriabin*: Prelude in D, and more!
00119742 / $8.99

First Grade

22 pieces: *Bartók*: A Conversation • *Mélanie Bonis*: Miaou! Ronron! • *Burgmüller*: Arabesque • *Handel*: Passepied • *d'Indy*: Two-Finger Partita • *Köhler*: Andantino • *Müller*: Lyric Etude • *Ryba*: Little Invention • *Schytte*: Choral Etude; Springtime • *Türk*: I Feel So Sick and Faint, and more!
00119738 / $6.99

The *Classical Piano Solos* series offers carefully-leveled, original piano works from Baroque to the early 20th century, featuring the simplest classics in Grade 1 to concert-hall repertoire in Grade 5. An assortment of pieces are featured, including familiar masterpieces by Bach, Beethoven, Mozart, Grieg, Schumann, and Bartók, as well as several lesser-known works by composers such as Melanie Bonis, Anatoly Lyadov, Enrique Granados, Vincent d'Indy, Theodor Kullak, and Samuel Coleridge-Taylor.

- Grades 1-4 are presented in a suggested order of study. Grade 5 is laid out chronologically.

- Features clean, easy-to-read engravings with clear but minimal editorial markings.

- View complete repertoire lists of each book along with sample music pages at **www.willispianomusic.com**.

The series was compiled to loosely correlate with the *John Thompson Modern Course*, but can be used with any method or teaching situation.

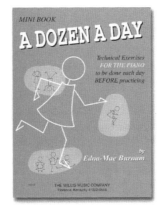